The Christmas Book

BY

MARCIA O. MARTIN

HUGH LAUTER LEVIN ASSOCIATES, INC., NEW YORK

DISTRIBUTED BY
THE SCRIBNER BOOK COMPANIES

ILLUSTRATIONS

Marcellus Coffermans
ADORATION OF THE SHEPHERDS
tempera and oil on wood
8⅛ × 5½"
Courtesy: The Metropolitan Museum of Art;
Gift of J. Pierpont Morgan, 1917

Norman Rockwell
DEAR SANTA
1935
Printed by permission of the Estate of Norman Rockwell
Copyright © 1935, Estate of Norman Rockwell
Photograph Courtesy: Harry N. Abrams, Inc.

David Armstrong
THE FARM, CHRISTMAS EVE
1980
watercolor
19 × 29"
Courtesy: Hammer Galleries

Guy Wiggins
NEW ENGLAND CHRISTMAS
1920
oil on masonite
32 × 32"
Private Collection
Photograph Courtesy: Kennedy Galleries, New York

Howard Sanden
CHRISTMAS VISITORS
undated
oil on canvas
30 × 39"
Collection of Robert Blattner
Photograph Courtesy: Walt Reed, Illustration House, Inc.

Stevan Dohanos
COVER OF THE SATURDAY EVENING POST,
December 13, 1947
Reprinted from THE SATURDAY EVENING POST
Copyright 1947, The Curtis Publishing Company

Fairfield Porter
INTERIOR WITH CHRISTMAS TREE
1971
color lithograph
25¼ × 22⅜"
Courtesy: Brooke Alexander, Inc., New York

J. Alden Weir
THE CHRISTMAS TREE
1890
Private Collection

THE NATIVITY (detail)
German, c. 1445
stained glass panel, Carmelite Church, Boppard-on-the-Rhine
41½ × 28½"
Courtesy: The Metropolitan Museum of Art;
Francis I. Leland Fund, 1913

Norman Rockwell
CHRISTMAS TRIO
1923
oil on board
28¼ × 21½"
Printed by permission of the Estate of Norman Rockwell
Copyright © 1923, Estate of Norman Rockwell
Photograph Courtesy: Harry N. Abrams, Inc.

Hieronymus Bosch
THE ADORATION OF THE MAGI
c. 1475–80
oil on wood
30½ × 22"
Courtesy: John G. Johnson Collection, Philadelphia

Thomas Nast
SANTA CLAUS
1874
Private Collection
Photograph Courtesy: Kennedy Galleries, New York

Norman Rockwell
FREEDOM FROM WANT
1943
oil on canvas
45¾ × 35½"
Printed by permission of the Estate of Norman Rockwell
Copyright © 1943, Estate of Norman Rockwell
Photography Courtesy: Harry N. Abrams, Inc.

Grandma Moses
CHRISTMAS AT HOME
1946
oil on pressed wood
18 × 23"
Private Collection
Copyright © 1982, Grandma Moses Properties Co., New York

Calligraphy by Gunta Alexander

Illustration research by Ann Levy

Editorial services by Harkavy Publishing Service

Printed in Japan

ISBN 0-88363-585-2

Page 18

Bundles
from SONGS FOR PARENTS by John Farrar, © Yale University
Press

Page 20

The Flight Into Egypt
from COLLECTED POEMS by W.H. Auden, edited by Edward
Mendelson, © Random House, Inc.

Page 30

Christmas
from STORIES TO BEGIN ON by Rhoda W. Bacmeister © 1940
by E.P. Dutton and Co., Inc., renewed 1968 by Rhoda W.
Bacmeister. Reprinted by permission of the publisher.

Page 40

We Sing of Life
by Percival Chubb. Permission granted by the American Ethical
Union. Copyright 1955 by The American Ethical Union Library
(Catalog number 54:11625).

Contents

Prologue

This book belongs to

_____

In this book we tell the story of five Christmases in our family. It contains memories of that December time when all of us once more relive the joys of the yuletide season.

Perhaps whoever picks up this book will share those memories and those joys and, in the spirit of the occasion, even carry on some of the traditions.

ADORATION OF THE SHEPHERDS—Marcellus Coffermans

The Story of the Nativity

The celebration of Christmas is, of course, the celebration of the birth of Jesus Christ. One of the most beautiful accounts of the Nativity is in the King James Version of the Bible.

And there were in the same country shepherds abiding in the field, keeping watch over their flock by night.

And, lo, the angel of the Lord came upon them, and the glory of the Lord shone round about them; and they were sore afraid.

And the angel said unto them, Fear not: for, behold, I bring you good tidings of great joy, which shall be to all people.

For unto you is born this day in the city of David a Savior, which is Christ the Lord.

And this shall be a sign unto you; Ye shall find the babe wrapped in swaddling clothes, lying in a manger.

And suddenly there was with the angel a multitude of the heavenly host praising God, and saying,

Glory to God in the highest, and on earth peace, good will toward men.

St. Luke
Chapter II, verses 8-14

In England, hanging mistletoe is a Christmas custom dating back to the ancient Druids.

In Ireland, often a special candle is placed in a window shortly after sunset on Christmas Eve.

In Italy, in a custom still practiced in Rome and in the Abruzzi region, bagpipers come down from the hills before Christmas and pass from house to house playing their music.

In Poland, children wait for the first star to appear on Christmas Eve, for this is their signal to begin the festivities.

In Germany, the traditional Christmas tree holds only white candles.

Family Christmas Traditions

Families have traditions, too. Some hang stockings on Christmas Eve; some have a visit from Santa Claus; some bake, sew, and build the gifts they give.

Below are a few of the preparations, trips, events, and customs that are a part of our family tradition:

_____

_____

_____

_____

_____

_____

_____

_____

_____

_____

Our Christmas Card List

Name   Address

DEAR SANTA—Norman Rockwell

Our Christmas Card List

Name   Address

Our Christmas Card List

Name   Address

_____

_____

_____

_____

_____

_____

_____

_____

_____

_____

_____

_____

_____

_____

_____

_____

_____

_____

_____

Pre-Christmas Preparations

Christmas 19___

Chill December brings the sleet,
Blazing fire and Christmas treat.
— Sara Coleridge

The Tree

Description _____

Where it was placed _____

When it was decorated _____

Who helped _____

_____

What was used _____

_____

_____

Other Decorations

What and where _____

_____

_____

_____

14

Christmas Eve

As Joseph was a-walking,
He heard an angel sing,
"This night shall be the birth-night
Of Christ our heavenly king."
— Old English carol

Weather _____

Where we spent the evening _____

_____

With whom _____

_____

_____

What we did _____

_____

_____

_____

_____

_____

15

Christmas Day

So now is come our joyful feast;
let every man be jolly.
Each room with ivy-leaves is dressed,
and every post with holly.
— George Wither

Weather _____

Where we spent the day _____

_____

With whom _____

_____

_____

What we did _____

_____

_____

_____

Christmas Dinner Menu

_____

_____

_____

16

THE FARM, CHRISTMAS EVE—David Armstrong

Christmas Gifts

A bundle is a funny thing,
It always sets me wondering...
Especially in Christmas week
Temptation is so great to peek!
—John Farrar

To Whom	From Whom	What

18

 # Christmas Gifts

To Whom	From Whom	What

19

Evergreen Thoughts

Well, so that is that. Now we must
dismantle the tree,
Putting the decorations back into
their cardboard boxes...

—W.H. Auden

So ends our first Christmas to be
recorded here. But these are some of the
special memories that will stay with us:

_____

_____

_____

_____

_____

_____

_____

_____

_____

_____

20

First Christmas, 19_____

NEW ENGLAND CHRISTMAS —*Guy Wiggins*

Christmas 19____

Christmas is coming,
the goose is getting fat;
Please to put a penny
in the old man's hat.
~Old English verse~

The Tree

Description_____

Where it was placed_____

When it was decorated_____

Who helped_____

_____

What was used_____

_____

_____

Other Decorations

What and where_____

_____

_____

22

Christmas Eve

The holly's up, the house is bright;
The tree is ready, candles alight;
Rejoice and be glad, all children tonight.
                                        —Peter Cornelius

Weather_____

Where we spent the evening_____

_____

With whom_____

_____

_____

_____

What we did_____

_____

_____

_____

_____

_____

23

May joy come from God above,
To all those who Christmas love.
—Thirteenth century carol

Weather _____

Where we spent the day _____

_____

With whom _____

_____

_____

What we did _____

_____

_____

_____

Christmas Dinner Menu

_____

_____

_____

Second Christmas, 19____

CHRISTMAS VISITORS—*Howard Sanden*

Christmas Gifts

On the first day of Christmas,
My true love gave to me
A partridge in a pear tree.
— Old English carol

To Whom	From Whom	What

Second Christmas, 19____

Christmas Gifts

To Whom	From Whom	What

Evergreen Thoughts

Down with the Rosemary, and so
Down with the Bays and the Mistletoe.
Down with the Holly, Ivy, all,
Wherewith we dressed the Christmas hall.

—Robert Herrick

Our second Christmas, as recorded here, has now ended. No two Christmases are alike, and there are memories of this one that should be shared as well.

_____

_____

_____

_____

_____

_____

_____

28

COVER OF THE SATURDAY EVENING POST—*Stevan Dohanos*

Pre-Christmas Preparations

Christmas 19___

Ring, bells, ring!
Sing, children, sing!
Christmas time has come again;
Ring, bells, ring!

—Rhoda Bacmeister

The Tree

Description _____

Where it was placed _____

When it was decorated _____

Who helped _____

_____

What was used _____

_____

_____

Other Decorations

What and where _____

_____

_____

30

Christmas Eve

Christmas where snow peaks stand solemn and white,
Christmas where cornfields lie sunny and bright;
Everywhere, everywhere Christmas tonight.
—Phillips Brooks

Weather _____

Where we spent the evening _____

_____

With whom _____

_____

_____

_____

What we did _____

_____

_____

_____

_____

_____

31

Christmas Day

At Christmas be merrie, and thankful withal;
And feast with thy neighbors, the great with the small.
                                        — Old English verse

Weather _____

Where we spent the day _____

_____

With whom _____

_____

_____

What we did _____

_____

_____

Christmas Dinner Menu

_____

_____

_____

32

INTERIOR WITH CHRISTMAS TREE—Fairfield Porter

Christmas Gifts

Hearts warmer grow,
Gifts freely flow,
For Christmas-time has come.
~ Louisa May Alcott

To Whom	From Whom	What

34

Christmas Gifts

To Whom	From Whom	What

Evergreen Thoughts

Now have good day, now have good day!
I am Christmas, and now I go my way!
—Balliol

Our third Christmas to be recorded in this book has come and gone. Still we are left with precious memories.

_____

_____

_____

_____

_____

_____

_____

_____

_____

36

THE CHRISTMAS TREE—J. Alden Weir

Pre-Christmas Preparations

Christmas 19___

Get ivy and holly, woman,
Deck up thine house.
— Thomas Tusser

The Tree

Description_____

Where it was placed_____

When it was decorated_____

Who helped_____

_____

What was used_____

_____

_____

Other Decorations

What and where_____

_____

_____

_____

38

Christmas Eve

On Christmas Eve the bells were rung;
On Christmas Eve the mass was sung.
—Sir Walter Scott

Weather _____

Where we spent the evening _____

_____

With whom _____

_____

_____

_____

What we did _____

_____

_____

_____

_____

_____

39

Fourth Christmas, 19____

Christmas Day

O we believe in Christmas
And we keep Christmas day;
And we will honor Christmas
The ancient world-wide way.
—Percival Chubb

Weather _____

Where we spent the day _____

_____

With whom _____

_____

_____

What we did _____

_____

_____

_____

Christmas Dinner Menu

_____

_____

_____

40

THE NATIVITY (detail)—German

Christmas Gifts

It is good to be children sometimes,
and none better than at Christmas.
— Charles Dickens

To Whom	From Whom	What

42

Christmas Gifts

To Whom	From Whom	What

43

Evergreen Thoughts

Yule's come, and Yule's gone,
And we hae feasted weel,
Sae Jock maun to his flail again,
And Jenny to her wheel.
~Anonymous

The memories of four Christmases are now preserved in this book. From this year's holiday time, here are a few of the thoughts that remain with us:

_____

_____

_____

_____

_____

_____

_____

_____

_____

_____

44

CHRISTMAS TRIO—*Norman Rockwell*

Pre-Christmas Preparations

Christmas 19___

Your Christmas comes with holly leaves
And snow about your door and eaves.

—John Runcie

The Tree

Description _____

Where it was placed _____

When it was decorated _____

Who helped _____

_____

What was used _____

_____

_____

Other Decorations

What and where _____

_____

_____

_____

46

Christmas Eve

Heap on more wood! – the wind is chill;
But let it whistle as it will,
We'll keep our Christmas merry still.
                                        —Sir Walter Scott

Weather _____

Where we spent the evening _____

_____

With whom _____

_____

_____

_____

What we did _____

_____

_____

_____

_____

_____

47

Christmas Day

Sing we all merrily,
Christmas is here,
The day we love best
Of all days in the year.
—Old English verse

Weather _____

Where we spent the day _____

_____

With whom _____

_____

_____

What we did _____

_____

_____

_____

Christmas Dinner Menu

_____

_____

_____

48

THE ADORATION OF THE MAGI—Hieronymus Bosch

 # Christmas Gifts

Not believe in Santa Claus!
You might as well not believe in fairies!
—Frank Church

To Whom	From Whom	What

50

Christmas Gifts

To Whom	From Whom	What

51

Evergreen Thoughts

We've celebrated Christmas
With peace, good-will to men;
And every year
With hearty cheer,
We'll celebrate again.
 —Old English rhyme

Though this fifth Christmas has come to an end, it will live on in our hearts and minds, along with some special thoughts written on this page:

_____

_____

_____

_____

_____

_____

_____

_____

_____

SANTA CLAUS—Thomas Nast

The cooks shall be busied by day and by night,
In roasting and boiling, for taste and delight...
They still are employed for to dress us, in brief,
Plum pudding, goose, capon, minc'd pies and roast beef.
—English ballad

Appetizers, Soups & Salads

_____

_____

_____

_____

_____

_____

_____

_____

_____

_____

_____

_____

_____

Vegetables, Aspics, & Relishes

Meat, Fish, & Fowl

FREEDOM FROM WANT—Norman Rockwell

Sauces, Stuffings, & Accompaniments

Our Favorite Christmas Recipes

Cookies, Cakes, Pies & Pastries

Beverages & Spirits

CHRISTMAS AT HOME—Grandma Moses

 # Guest Register

The greeting given, the music played
In honor of each household name,
Duly pronounced with lusty call,
And "Merry Christmas" wished to all!

—William Wordsworth

Date	Name	Address	Comments

 # Guest Register

Date	Name	Address	Comments

This book tells the story of five of our special Christmases and how we have celebrated them with joy, and reverence, with giving and receiving, with family and friends in the spirit of the season.

"It was always said of him that he knew how to keep Christmas well...May that truly be said of us, and all of us! And so, as Tiny Tim observed,

God Bless Us,
Every One."

— Charles Dickens